Custodians

Julie Murray

BARTHOLOMEW
COUNTY PUBLIC LIBRARY
COLUMBUS, INDIANA 47201

Abdo Kids Junior
is an Imprint of Abdo Kids
abdobooks.com

MY COMMUNITY: JOBS

abdobooks.com

Published by Abdo Kids, a division of ABDO, P.O. Box 398166, Minneapolis, Minnesota 55439. Copyright © 2021 by Abdo Consulting Group, Inc. International copyrights reserved in all countries. No part of this book may be reproduced in any form without written permission from the publisher. Abdo Kids Junior™ is a trademark and logo of Abdo Kids.

Printed in the United States of America, North Mankato, Minnesota.

102020
012021 987-2638

THIS BOOK CONTAINS RECYCLED MATERIALS

Photo Credits: Alamy, Getty Images, iStock, Media Bakery, Shutterstock

Production Contributors: Teddy Borth, Jennie Forsberg, Grace Hansen

Design Contributors: Candice Keimig, Dorothy Toth

Library of Congress Control Number: 2020910585
Publisher's Cataloging-in-Publication Data

Names: Murray, Julie, author.
Title: Custodians / by Julie Murray
Description: Minneapolis, Minnesota : Abdo Kids, 2021 | Series: My community: jobs | Includes online resources and index.
Identifiers: ISBN 9781098205799 (lib. bdg.) | ISBN 9781098206352 (ebook) | ISBN 9781098206635 (Read-to-Me ebook)
Subjects: LCSH: Janitors--Juvenile literature. | Community life--Juvenile literature. | Occupations--Juvenile literature. | Cities and towns--Juvenile literature.
Classification: DDC 647.2--dc23

Table of Contents

Custodians............4

A Custodian's
Tools...............22

Glossary...........23

Index..............24

Abdo Kids Code.....24

Custodians

Jake is a custodian.

He loves his job!

Tom keeps buildings clean and safe.

Mae works at a school.

She mops the floors.

The door handle is broken.

Jay fixes it.

Zach works in an office.

He empties the **recycling**.

The light is out. Cleo changes the bulb.

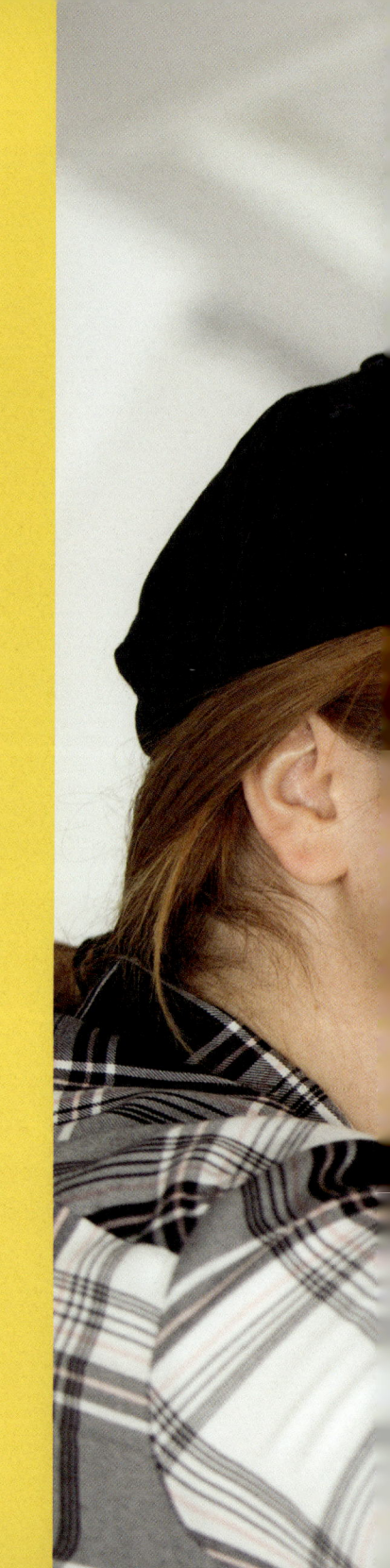

15

Gus cleans the windows.

Ali works at a hotel. She **vacuums** the floor.

Do you know a custodian?

21

A Custodian's Tools

ladder

mop

toolbox

vacuum

Glossary

recycling
waste material set aside to be recycled.

vacuum
or vacuum cleaner, an electrical appliance that cleans floors.

Index

cleaning 6, 8, 16, 18

light bulbs 14

mop 8

recycling 12

repairs 10

safety 6

vacuum 18

windows 16

Visit **abdokids.com** to access crafts, games, videos, and more!

Use Abdo Kids code **MCK5799** or scan this QR code!

7/2021   1.2